DATE DUE

JAN 1 2 1984		
MAY 8 1984		
NOV 9 84		
JAN 9 1996		
MAR 2 '89		
MAR 1 3 '92		
MAY 1 3 '92		
GAYLORD		PRINTED IN U.S.A

Sport Stars

RENALDO NEHEMIAH

Bionic Hurdler

By Don Pierson

 **CHILDRENS PRESS, CHICAGO**

Picture Acknowledgments

Cover photograph: Focus on Sports inc
Inside photographs courtesy of the following: Geoff Baker, pages 6,
8 (bottom), 11, 16, 18, 20, 23, 28, 32, and 34;
Howard Zryb, pages 14 and 42; University of Maryland, pages 8 (top) and 25;
Wide World Photos, pages 30 and 37; and UPI, page 41.

Library of Congress Cataloging in Publication Data

Pierson, Don, 1944—
    Renaldo Nehemiah: bionic hurdler.

    (Sports stars)
    SUMMARY: Examines the record-setting career in
running hurdles of Renaldo Nehemiah.
    1. Nehemiah, Renaldo, 1959—   —Juvenile
literature. 2. Track and field athletes—United
States—Biography—Juvenile literature.
[1. Nehemiah, Renaldo, 1959—   2. Track and
field athletes] I. Title. II. Series.
GV697.N43P53   796.4′2′0924 [B] [92]   79-22112
ISBN 0-516-04308-0

1 2 3 4 5 6 7 8 9 10 11 12 R 87 86 85 84 83 82 81 80

Sport Stars

RENALDO NEHEMIAH

Bionic Hurdler

Skeets is one of the fastest runners in the world.

Renaldo "Skeets" Nehemiah became the best hurdler in the world. He was 19 years old. Now he wants to go to the Olympic Games. In 1980 they will be in Moscow. He wants to win a gold medal. He never has been in the Olympic Games.

"Everything I do is aimed for the Olympics," says Nehemiah.

Nehemiah got his nickname "Skeets" when he was a baby. His uncle saw him crawl around his house in Scotch Plains, New Jersey. He called him "Skeets."

"He seemed to be running," says Renaldo's father, Earl Nehemiah.

"It's because you have to be a skeet shooter to catch me," laughs Renaldo. (A skeet shooter shoots at clay targets that imitate the flight of a bird.)

Almost everybody calls him Skeets now. Hardly anyone calls him by his real first name, Renaldo.

Skeets is a very fast runner. He is one of the fastest runners in the world. But he does more than run. He jumps over hurdles. His race is 110-meters long. That is a little longer than a football field. There are 10 hurdles. Each hurdle is 10 yards apart. Each hurdle is 42 inches high. That's as tall as a five-year-old child.

Skeets runs fast. It takes him less than a quarter of a second to jump over each hurdle. If you blink your eyes, you might miss him. The hurdles is a hard race to learn. But Skeets makes it look easy. He has set many world records in the hurdles.

Nehemiah likes to be the best at whatever he does.

He used to run in street races in his neighborhood. He said, "It meant a lot for me to win, particularly if there were people watching. I always wanted to do well in front of people, to be the winner and have everyone notice me."

When Nehemiah was 10 years old, his father started teaching him football. He taught his younger son Dion too. Dion is two years younger than Renaldo. Renaldo also has a sister named Lisa. She is four years younger.

Running in the 100-meter dash.

Nehemiah played football well. He scored 13 touchdowns for a club team. But football wasn't the only thing he played.

When he was 11, Skeets started playing the alto saxophone. Why did he choose the saxophone? For the same reason he later chose hurdles instead of another race. It was a challenge.

"The trumpet has three valves. On a trombone you just slide up and down. It didn't seem like anything," Nehemiah said. "But all those keys on a saxophone were a challenge."

Renaldo won a scholarship to a summer music school. He was in the seventh grade.

Mr. Nehemiah bought his children all kinds of sports equipment. When everybody else was wearing sneakers, Skeets had a pair of expensive running shoes.

One time, Mr. Nehemiah wanted all three of his children to learn karate. Dion was the best. He became an instructor with a black belt rating. Renaldo quit karate so he could run track. But Lisa remembers Skeets' first karate class. "The very first time he hit a board, he broke it in half," she says.

Skeets also played baseball. He was in Little League. Skeets would get on first base. Then he would steal both second and third base on the first pitch. He was too fast for the catcher to throw him out at second. Finally, the catchers got smart. They threw the ball to third when he was stealing second. This was the only way they could get him out.

When Skeets was in seventh grade, he went out for track. He didn't like it very much. He had to run too far. "It was introduced to me as building endurance, putting in mileage, and I quit," he said.

He didn't come out again until the ninth grade. At first he wanted to be a sprinter. But he didn't think he was fast enough. "I didn't want to lose in the 100-yard dash. So I tried the hurdles for something different," he says. "I liked them right away. I got banged up a few times, but I was determined. My coach told me one day I would be state champion."

In high school, the hurdles are only 39 inches tall. Still, this was high. Renaldo was only 66 inches tall.

Skeets set school records in the ninth grade. He practiced his form at home. He would hurdle over a bed while looking into a mirror. He was looking forward to the rest of his high school career. But he had bad luck.

Skeets tore a hamstring muscle in his leg. He had to use crutches. He couldn't run at all. "I'd have to stand in the classroom. It was too painful to sit. I used to sit in my room at night and cry. It used to tear me apart to stand on the sidelines. I'd watch guys I knew I could beat on the hurdles," he said.

Skeets talks to teammate Greg Robertson before an indoor meet.

But this made him all the more determined. His mother had died of lung cancer earlier. He had felt the same determination then.

"I was always the closest to her," said Skeets. "My brother and sister were more with my father. She's always in the back of my mind. Everything I do—not letting up, wanting to go to the top, to be the best—is done with the thought of how happy she'd be if she were alive to see it."

Mr. Nehemiah remarried. Now Renaldo has a stepmother. The Nehemiahs are a close family. "We do a lot together," says Lisa. "If one of us is participating in sports activities or anything, we all go to watch. We take trips together and go to church together as a family."

The University of Maryland wins many meets because of Skeets.

Nehemiah set a New Jersey state record in the 120-yard high hurdles. He was a junior in high school then. That race is only 10.7 inches shorter than 110 meters. Skeets ran it in 13.6 seconds.

"That was a real boost to me," he said.

As a senior at Scotch Plains-Fanwood High School, Nehemiah was quarterback of the football team. He was six feet tall.

Track was still his main sport. And he soon showed why. He set state records in the 100-yard dash, the 220-yard dash, and the long jump. In the hurdles, he set national records.

"He broke records," said his coach, Larry Thomas, ". . . no, he *destroyed* records."

He ran the 330-yard intermediate hurdles (36 inches high) in 35.8 seconds. He ran his specialty, the 120-yard highs, in 12.9 seconds. It was the first time any hurdler had been timed in under 13 seconds for 120 yards or 110 meters, over high school or standard hurdles.

"In the middle of the race, I suddenly became aware of my speed. It was more like a sprint," said Nehemiah. "Actually, I hit the seventh hurdle or I could have run faster."

In the 60-yard high hurdles. Skeets wins in 6.9 seconds.

Most high school hurdlers have trouble running in college. The hurdles are three inches higher. But Renaldo had been practicing with 42-inch hurdles in high school. Sometimes he even practiced with 45-inch hurdles.

Nehemiah goes to the University of Maryland. He is studying accounting and business. He started running during the indoor track season. Indoors, the races are shorter. Most of them are 60 yards. They have only five hurdles. Renaldo lost his first two races his freshman year in college. But he won his last seven indoors.

Outdoors, he ran well. But he lost two races to Greg Foster of U.C.L.A. Foster was a year older.

In the national college championships, Foster beat Nehemiah. Foster set an American record of 13.22. It broke the record set by 1972 Olympic champion Rod Milburn.

The United States has had many great hurdlers. They have won 15 out of 18 Olympic gold medals. Milburn was one of the greatest. Nehemiah wanted to become another Milburn.

"Everything I do is patterned after him," said Nehemiah. He was upset that Greg Foster broke Milburn's record.

The next week there was a national meet. It was for runners in college and out of college. Nehemiah beat Foster. But the time was 13.28. This was not as fast as Foster had run.

Both hurdlers went to Europe to compete. They met four times. Nehemiah won every time. But he couldn't run as fast as 13.22.

Track and Field News ranked Nehemiah the No. 1 hurdler in the world for 1978. He was only 19 years old. Foster was No. 2. Some people thought Foster would someday be better.

In their first indoor race in 1979, Nehemiah beat Foster again. Then Nehemiah set a world record in the 60-yard hurdles. His record was 7.02 seconds. Foster wasn't in the race.

The next time they met, they tied. They both set another world record of 6.95.

"There can't be two No. 1s," said Nehemiah. The next night, he beat Foster. He set still another world record of 6.89. Foster didn't race against him again indoors.

Nehemiah went on to set world records for 50 yards and 50 meters.

"I want the hurdles to be the glamour event of track, like the mile," said Nehemiah. Many people came to watch him race. "I like the attention," he said. "Track is the most beautiful sport to watch. It's the human body doing something by itself. The hurdles are a beautiful race, fast and smooth. Not everyone can jump over a hurdle and keep their balance. You have to have speed, coordination, and strength to run the hurdles."

Skeets gives the No. 1 sign after winning the 110-meter hurdles in 13.19 seconds.

Sometimes Nehemiah sounds like he's bragging.

"He doesn't have a big head at all," says his college coach, Frank Costello. "He may mention he's No. 1. But in his sport, that's a fact, not a boast."

"He cares about people. He's not selfish. He's just like one of the guys. Never acts like anyone special," says his teammate at Maryland, Greg Robertson.

The world record for the 110-meter hurdles was 13.21. It was set by Cuba's Alberto Casanas in 1977.

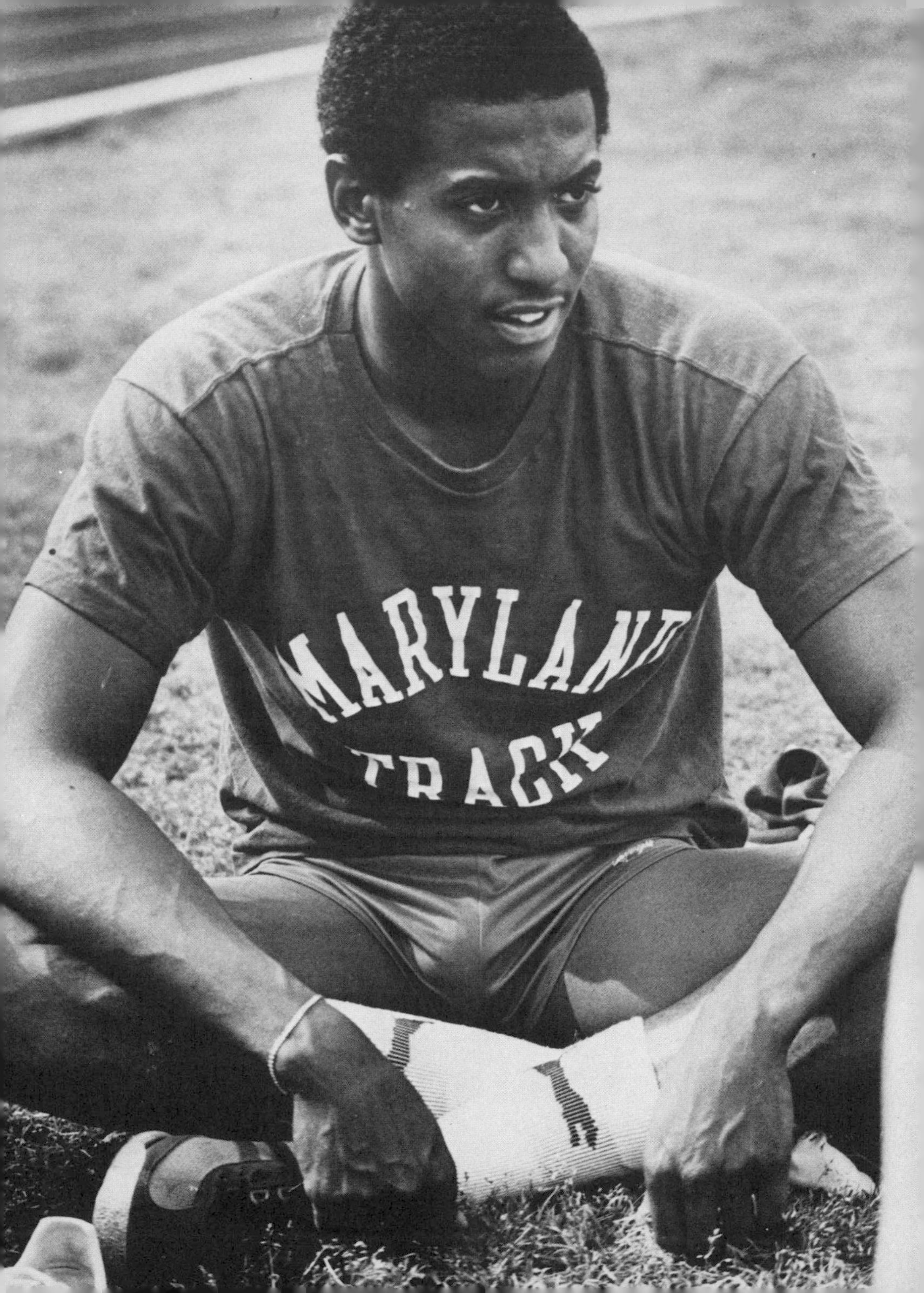
TRACK

Nehemiah said he would break it. "If I don't go under 13.1, it will be a slap in the face," he said.

In his first outdoor race of 1979, he broke Casanas' record. He ran a 13.16.

"If Greg Foster had been here, I think I could have gone even faster," he said. Nehemiah had just turned 20 years old.

Now he was the fastest hurdler who ever lived. But something still bothered him. Some of his friends were kidding him. They told him all he could do was run one short hurdles race. They were sprinters who had to run more. They ran 200 meters and 400 meters. They thought they had to practice harder and longer than Nehemiah did.

Nehemiah wanted to show them. He did, in the Penn Relays. This is one of the country's biggest track meets.

He ran three relays with his teammates. In the hurdles relay, his team was behind. Then it was Nehemiah's turn to run. He passed everybody. Maryland won easily.

In another relay, he had to run 200 meters without hurdles. His team was behind again. This time it would be harder to catch up. But he did. So Maryland won another trophy. There were 23,000 people watching. They knew they had seen something special.

Next, he had to run 400 meters in another relay. "I didn't want to run it. I was hurting so bad after the 200," Nehemiah said. But he did. This time his team was so far behind no one thought he had a chance.

"I was mentally down when I got the baton," said Skeets. "I knew the other guys in the race could run the 400 in 45 seconds. I was just going to try and close the gap a little." He had run 400 meters before. His fastest was 46.2 seconds.

Nehemiah started to catch the two runners in front of him. Halfway through the race, he was still more than 10 meters behind. No one thought he could win.

Suddenly, Skeets started running very fast. It looked like he had shifted gears.

"I don't have much experience, so I didn't know what to expect," he said. "I had all this extra energy. The last 110 meters felt like my first 110."

He won the race. He was timed in 44.3 seconds. The fans were very surprised. They stood and cheered for five minutes.

"I get a lot of flak from athletes saying 100 yards isn't anything. I wanted to show them I do more than just sprint in practice. I wanted to show I could contend outside the hurdles," he said.

"The guy's bionic, you know?" said Costello.

The next week he ran the hurdles. He ran against both Foster and Casanas. Everyone expected big things.

Casanas had a false start. The race was started over. Again, Casanas looked like he false-started. But the race went on.

Foster and Nehemiah were left in the starting blocks.

"I panicked," said Nehemiah. "I really had to dig down and go after him."

Foster lost his balance. He fell down at the fourth hurdle.

Nehemiah finally caught Casanas by the sixth hurdle. He passed him and won the race. He waited for the announcer to give the time. It was 13 seconds flat, another world record.

Nehemiah beat Foster in two more races. This was before the national college meet. Nehemiah wanted to win the nationals badly. Foster had won the year before.

Foster was ready to defend his championship. But Nehemiah beat him. The time was 12.91. A wind was blowing too hard for it to be a record. Foster fell again. He said the wind bothered him.

"I already have the world record, so I'm satisfied," said Nehemiah. "I'm glad I went 12.91, wind or not."

In 13 seconds flat Skeets beat Casanas and set a world record.

"Skeets is the best in the world. He has to prove it every time out," said coach Costello.

"I have to win. I have no choice," he says. "No one will accept anything less. I've spoiled the public. And I've spoiled myself. It's a thrill to try and better myself.

"I want to do the impossible. I've never wanted to be a contender, just one of the crowd. I want to be someone who turns the event around, who goes out and explores new territory."

RENALDO NEHEMIAH

CHRONOLOGY

1959 — Renaldo Nehemiah is born on March 24.

1969 — At the age of 10, "Skeets" scores 13 touchdowns for a club football team.

1970 — Skeets starts playing the saxophone.

1972 — In seventh grade, Skeets goes out for track, but doesn't like it.

1974 — Skeets comes out for track in ninth grade and tries the hurdles. He likes the event.

1977 — In his senior year at Scotch Plains-Fanwood High School in New Jersey, Nehemiah set national high school records of 35.8 in the 330-yard intermediate hurdles and 12.9 in the 120-yard high hurdles.

1978 — As a freshman at the University of Maryland, Skeets won 19 of 24 hurdles races in the United States and Europe and was ranked No. 1 in the world by *Track and Field News*.

1979

Jan. — Set world records for 55-meter hurdles and 60-yard hurdles.

Feb. — Set world records for 50-meter hurdles, 50-yard hurdles, and 60-meter hurdles.

Apr. — Set world record for 110-meter hurdles of 13.16.

May — Set another world record for 110-meter hurdles of 13.00.

June — Won NCAA title in 110-meter hurdles in wind-aided 12.91.
     — Won AAU title in 110-meter hurdles in 13.19.

ABOUT THE AUTHOR

Don Pierson has covered a variety of sports in his career as a writer. He has covered the Chicago Bears for 10 years as a reporter for the *Chicago Tribune*. He has covered Cubs and White Sox games, Super Bowls, tennis, and Big Ten football and basketball. He wrote a book on University of Southern California football.

But his favorite sport is track and field. A past president of the Track and Field Writers of America, Mr. Pierson has covered Olympic trials, national and international meets, and local track. Never has he seen a more spectacular athletic performance than the year hurdler Renaldo Nehemiah had in 1979.